CRAZY FOR CATS

The criteria which I have used in the drafting of this book have been scientific truth, and imagination, which are more similar to each other than people commonly think

O.S.

CRAZY FOR CATS

Orietta Sala
Illustrations by
Claudine Titeca

Anaya Publishers
London

First published in Great Britain in 1990 by Anaya Publishers Ltd
49 Neal Street, London WC2H 9PJ

Originally published in Italy in 1989
by Idealibri S.p.A., via San Tomaso, 10, Milano

Copyright © Idealibri S.p.A. 1989
Translation copyright © Anaya Publishers Ltd 1990

Translated from the Italian by Sue Wason

All rights reserved. No part of this publication may be reproduced, stored in a retrieval system, or transmitted, in any form or by any means, electronic, mechanical, photocopying, recording or otherwise, without the permission of the copyright holder.

ISBN 1–85470–022–7

British Library Cataloguing in Publication Data
A CIP catalogue record for this book is available from the British Library

Photocomposition by Speedset Ltd, Ellesmere Port
Printed and bound in Italy

CONTENTS

INTRODUCTION
6

SAM
8

WHISKERS
10

TOM, DICK AND HARRY
12

TONTON GASTON
14

BONBON, PUFF,
HAMLET
AND BISCUIT
17

PHILIP
20

HAROLD
22

MARMALADE CATS
24

GINGER AND TIGGER
27

WALRUS AND THE SMITS FAMILY
30

LADY LUSTI VON MIMOSEN
32

ANNA LISA
34

DAISY AND HER KITTENS
36

BILLY
38

TALKING HEADS
40

POLO AND PEPPERMINT
42

LOTS OF CATS
44

PHILIP AND THE BARN OWL
46

ROMA AND JULIUS
49

FURRY BEAR
52

CRAZY FOR CATS

INTRODUCTION

To live without at least one cat in the house means living without imagination, happiness or tenderness. It means depriving yourself of their reassuring company, their natural elegance and the ineffable sense of calm and delight which a cat expresses with its whole being.

The author of this book would not know how to manage without this appealing animal. A breath, a twitch, a yawn. . . . A soft purr, a conspiratorial miaow, a sudden pricking of the ears. . . . A tail caressing you, a game of strength, a bejewelled glance, indecipherable, but apparently fixed on a secret horizon. . . .

Claudine paints, and paints only cats: her artistic world has restricted her to those creatures wandering regally about her house full of playthings, in and out of her studio crowded with colours, round the huge garden which dominates a sea of hills.

Orietta has a maternal and educative vocation: her cats give birth one after the other, and there is always a great deal to do to help them; to wean the little ones, to find homes for them with the right friends and to make sure that the moods of cats and guests do not enter into conflict.

Her affection and her kindness are never overpowering, and still less possessive, nor could they be, seeing that they are addressed to animals who have made independence and dignity their dominant characteristics.

Both ladies live happily with their cats and love them to the point of wanting to paint their portraits with words and brushes. Here are Lusti, Tonton Gaston, Billy, Philip, Daisy . . . with all their whims, desires and obsessions, and here are many other cats as well, familiar to you, and loved by you.

It is because they all have that special dimension which derives from the very essence of cat, that 'superb catness' which man absolutely lacks, that arcane hypnotic power, that mixture of idol and magic, of wild ferocity and sublime contemplative indolence which fascinates us so much.

Curled up on the drawing-room cushions, motionless at the edge of a wood, stretched out in the shade of the lavender bush, intent on a game which only he knows . . . he holds his mystery within him. Is it worth trying to snatch it from him? Perhaps not. And yet. . . .

M. S.

CRAZY FOR CATS

S A M

You mustn't pull Sam's whiskers
'Twould be an awful sin
You mustn't make him frightened
Or lift him by the chin
For cats with runny noses
Will jump out of their skin

* * *

Sam, like all cats, has a patch on each side of his nose, pierced by elegant little dots from which grow his long whiskers. When they are erect, they describe a circumference which is bigger than the volume of his body. They contain a very fine nervous system, are connected to small muscles, and they have the same function as the antennae of a butterfly (to which Sam is linked by sympathy which has nothing to do with alimentary interests).

Such a rudimentary but effective radar apparatus allows a precise exploration of reality. It serves to warn of obstacles, to sense a quarry, to measure the width of a hole through which to escape if chased by a large and fierce animal. The dimension of the hole will always correspond to this calculation: if the whiskers can get through, then so will the rest of the body. It is absolutely inadvisable to cut or pluck Sam's whiskers or to interfere with them in any way. It's unsuitable in every sense and contrary to all rules of hygiene and good manners.

The Snake Game
This gives great pleasure and is perfect for moments of relaxation. Slowly stroke the whiskers backwards over the shape of the head. The cat will stretch out in ecstasy and become as long as a snake.

CRAZY FOR CATS

WHISKERS

Let me sink into your beautiful eyes of metal and agate

(Charles Baudelaire)

* * *

We all have cones and rods in the retina of our eyes, but we don't all have the *tapetum lucidum*. Cats do. Its name literally means carpet, and it covers the retina. At night when struck by rays of light, it reflects it, creating a phosphorescent phenomenon. It is very useful, especially for nocturnal animals who do not possess navigation lights or anti-dazzle lamps. But it is untrue that cats see in an extraordinary way in darkness: they can only distinguish the outlines of objects, and with the help of their whiskers they can avoid obstacles.

Moreover, they also have the nictitating membrane and the dilating pupil. The nictitating membrane, as strange as its name, is a third eyelid, hidden in the lower corner of the eye, towards the nose. It serves as a window cleaner when the eye needs cleaning, it protects the eye from knocks, and distributes tears correctly. However, if, instead of remaining hidden, it should appear and cover even a small part of the cornea, you should take the cat straight to the vet, because it can be a sign of dangerous illness.

Having dilating pupils is very practical too, so that instead of having to buy himself sunglasses, Whiskers can constrict his pupils right down to a slit when there is a lot of light, and can make them as round as a ball again when there is only a little.

However, cat's eyes are very beautiful, not to say exquisite. Poets have marvelled at them: mystic pupils, glints of gold, bright lamps, 'living opals' (Baudelaire), 'glorious eyes that smile and burn' (Swinburne), 'languid pupils of green gold' (Huysmans), 'changing eyes like the changing moon' (Yeats), and still more; of sapphire and topaz, green fire, of the devil, almond-like, reflecting the light of the stars and, naturally, the mirror of the soul.

CRAZY FOR CATS

TOM, DICK AND HARRY

The cat who travels far and wide
Is the cat who'll be the perfect guide
In Greece he'll see the Parthenon
In France he'll visit the cyclotron
He'll cross the seas to Argentina
And even visit St Helena

* * *

Tom, Dick and Harry are very well acquainted with Robert Louis Stevenson's famous expression 'To travel hopefully is a better thing than to arrive'. In fact, they do know when they are leaving, but they know neither the day, nor their destination. Curious, and attracted by even the most imperceptible presence or smell, they are constantly stopping along the way. A journey in a hot air balloon would therefore have its advantages, with no prearranged stops, proceeding inexorably in an unplanned direction. (The only thing that could interrupt the journey would be a technological or meteorological catastrophe.)

Tom, Dick and Harry, had they been accustomed to much change since they were kittens, would pursue into adulthood their love for great moves, on condition that they were accompanied by their loved one.

Left in one place for a long time, they grow lazy, and develop a tendency to consider an unknown destination as a source of probable unhappiness. Transported as adults against their wishes, they can refuse to accept the move, and return to the point of departure, even when it involves huge distances (up to 2,000 miles).

How they manage this is a cause of some amazement and has been the subject of many scientific experiments. Some consider that in some mechanical way the route is registered in the brain, though no one knows how, and anyway, there is always the possibility that they return by a different route, or use short cuts. Perhaps it is simply a matter of sheer luck. Or of many patient attempts until they finally find the right street.

Crazy for Cats

TONTON GASTON

Cat! Who hast pass'd thy grand climacteric
How many mice and rats hast in thy days
Destroyed? How many titbits stolen? Gaze,
With those bright languid segments green, and prick
Those velvet ears — but pr'ythee do not stick
Thy latent talons in me — and upraise
Thy gentle mew — and tell me all thy frays
Of fish and mice, and rats and tender chick.

(John Keats)

On his birthday Tonton Gaston likes to be served at table. He has received a gift of a red rose, two lobsters and a pheasant.

He likes fish, asparagus tips and ice cream. He is not supposed to eat the meat of the pig, but on special occasions he hugely enjoys an ounce or two of cooked ham. His normal diet is minced beef, chicken and veal, raw or boiled liver and heart, and boiled fish carefully mixed with rice or potatoes. Don't forget a vegetable or two — courgette, beans, onion, carrot, cabbage or certain herbs when his health demands it. Even carnivores need vitamins. It is nevertheless sensible to consult the party concerned, and in any case never try to apply moral principles.

Gaston likes to have his friend beside him while he eats, because dining alone is always miserable. He usually likes to taste what is being served at table, with the exception of Béarnaise sauce and beetroot, but he is always happy to accept cheese, butter, roasts and omelettes.

CRAZY FOR CATS

TONTON GASTON

**Birthday Dinner
for Tonton Gaston**
*To start:
Little cubes of jellied chicken stock
Scrambled eggs with cheese
Main course:
Meatballs and corned tongue
For dessert:
Smoked salmon
or Norwegian gravadlax
To finish:
Warm milk*

The phrase 'eat when you are hungry' is applicable only to children, not to Tonton Gaston (nor indeed is it applicable to dogs who eat everything at once with irrepressible greed). Tonton Gaston would go without food for several days rather than eat something he doesn't like.

His motto is: Giving in to overwhelming hunger will not change the world.

BONBON, PUFF, HAMLET AND BISCUIT AT SCHOOL

Kittens, cats and tom cats too
Aren't born the way they seem
They need a little schooling
Though nothing too extreme
They're not too fond of algebra
They don't find Latin nice
The sciences they just accept
Especially those of mice

Lessons in Zoology take place out of doors. Particular attention is given to the magpie, which is eyecatchingly dressed in black and white, and is interesting because, like the wagtail, it prefers walking to flying. Then the lesson turns to recognition of the squirrel, so as not to confuse it with the rabbit, which is much more common in fields. In warm countries our feline friends discover that lizards contain neither vitamins nor proteins, and if swallowed will induce vomiting. Yet the game of the detachable tail which wriggles, to which such animals meekly subject themselves, is very enjoyable, especially for the little ones at nursery school. Green or red lizards have a tremendous bite. Bear in mind that bees and wasps sting too, especially on the cheeks, when one tries to sniff them.

Feline Intelligence
To those who express doubts about the intelligence of the cat, and its capacity to memorize, scientists have responded with the following experiment.

BONBON, PUFF, HAMLET AND BISCUIT AT SCHOOL

Put a cat under a bell jar and create a vacuum by sucking away all the air with a tube connected to a pump. The cat will fall into a faint. Proceed to revive it and after a while repeat the operation. As soon as the cat realizes that the pump is in motion, it will immediately block the opening of the tube with its paw, preventing withdrawal of air.

CRAZY FOR CATS

PHILIP

*The Owl and the Pussycat went to sea
In a beautiful pea-green boat.
They took some honey and plenty of money,
Wrapped up in a five-pound note.*
                              (Edward Lear)

* * *

Other famous sayings
The Cat, He walked by himself, and all places were alike to him.
                              (Rudyard Kipling)

Curiosity killed the cat.

When the cat's away the mice will play.

To put the cat among the pigeons.

A cat can be your friend, but never your slave.
                              (Théophile Gautier)

The cat's whiskers

If you want to write, keep cats.
                              (Aldous Huxley)

The cat has absolute emotional honesty.
                              (Ernest Hemingway)

There is, indeed, no single quality of the cat that man could not emulate to his advantage.
                              (Carl van Vechten)

Better one cat today than no cats tomorrow.

There's no room to swing a cat.

Cats are the tigers of us poor devils.
                              (Théophile Gautier)

A home without a cat, and a well-fed, well-petted and properly revered cat, may be a perfect home, perhaps, but how can it prove its title?
                              (Mark Twain)

Crazy for Cats

HAROLD

*I have seen
how the cat trembles
while sleeping
The night runs over him
like dark water*

(Pablo Neruda)

* * *

Sleep is sacred. Legend tells how Mohammed preferred to cut off the sleeve of his robe upon which his cat Muezza was sleeping rather than disturb him. Mohammed was a sensitive person. Let's hope that others will follow his enlightened example.

Harold's delicate nervous system means that he needs at least twelve hours' rest every day. In fact, he spends up to two-thirds of his life asleep.

The choice of a place to sleep requires attention, reasoning and imagination. The essential elements to consider, apart from, of course, security, are comfort, which often means luxury, beauty, tidiness and silence: qualities which Harold likes in particular. So his preference will be for the soft cushion, the precious fur, the chintz armchair cosily placed by the fireside, the bed of soft leaves, and all sorts of new objects of promising appearance: the piece of paper still wet with ink, the newly ironed silk shirt, and anything into which it is possible to enter: boxes, handbags, baskets, chests, cartons — any mysterious dark cavity demands instant exploration.

Before going to sleep Harold turns on his noise selector switchboard. This distinguishes the familiar from the unfamiliar and the terribly suspicious. He will not bother to wake up for the former, but for the last two he will immediately open his eyes, prick up his ears and be ready to leap.

When the need for sleep is urgent as well as being sacred, there are ingenious ways to procure it. Late at night, when Charles Dickens's cat Wilhelmina was fed up with hearing the scratching of her master's quill pen, she would resolutely extinguish his candle with her paw, to prevent him working any longer.

MARMALADE CATS

Marmalade cats
Are ginger and white.
They're quick and they're lively
And ever so bright.
And though it is said
That they're ruled by their head
They're brilliant at football and dancing and bed.

         * * *

Marmalade cats
Never need sleep.
They seem to have lost their tails and their feet
They fill their lives with romance and passion
And keep in a bunch – it's only a fashion.

Crazy for Cats

MARMALADE CATS

Into this category come Orlando the Marmalade cat, Puss in Boots, and the Cheshire Cat from *Alice in Wonderland*, who disappears beginning with his tail, until all that remains is his grin. 'A grin without a cat! It's the most curious thing I ever saw in all my life!' cries Alice.

All cats have a bit of the wizard in them: we never know where they are going or what they are doing. We do not know what they are thinking, while they know exactly what is in our shopping bag, and what we intend to buy tomorrow; most mysterious of all, they always know when we are leaving.

And they have a history. What history do dogs have? And all we know about the cow is that it jumped over the moon.

In ancient Egypt cats were considered divine. When they died they were embalmed like the Pharoahs, and mummified along with mice mummies for company. Near the ruins of the ancient city of Beni Hassan a burial ground was discovered containing more than three hundred thousand mummified cats. The Japanese considered cats good luck charms, and the Arabs believed them to be pure, in contrast to man. It was only in Catholic countries that, defined as messengers of the devil and familiars of witches, they were cruelly persecuted.

GINGER AND TIGGER

Dear James Thurber,
Our cat, who is 35 years old, spends most of his time in bed. His eyes follow my every move and this is beginning to get on my nerves. He is never sleepy and does not seem at all happy. What can I give him?

Miss L. Mc

* * *

Dear Miss L. Mc
There are no medicines which can be administered without risk to your cat, as far as procuring him happiness; all the same, you could try lettuce as a soporific. However, I would have to see the animal to diagnose whether anything can be done in order to turn his attention elsewhere.

Yours
James Thurber

Herbs help to balance the diet and prevent illness. So said Dioscorides, Hippocrates and Galen. Herbs and plants can be ground up and added to the food or infused and added by spoonful to each meal. Products based on micronized herbs mixed with pleasant-tasting flour can be found in specialist chemists.

For liver problems, lack of appetite, poisoning, problems of a sedentary life
Herbs rich in the bitter principles which favour the production of bile and the purification of the blood: dandelion, parsley, onion, cooked leek and carrot, spinach (known as the broom of the intestine).

For obesity, excess cholesterol, rheumatic problems and disorders of the skin
Diuretic, antitoxic and anti-rheumatic plants: infusion of elm bark or tender limewood or ash leaves.

For intestinal parasites
Vermifugal plants: camomile or tansy flowers (boiled in a tiny amount of

GINGER AND TIGGER

water and administered together with the water), ground raw garlic (one clove).

For diarrhoea
Astringent plants: nettles, an infusion of young oak roots, carob pulp, apple purée.

For hysterical pregnancy (caused by problems with the hormonal cycle) and other female disorders
Emmenagogic plants to regulate the cycle: marigold flowers, hops, leaves and flower tips of sage.

For eczema and skin conditions
Soothing, disinfectant and healing herbs (applied locally): infusion of thyme, pennyroyal or lavender flowers, poultice of nasturtium flowers, comfrey root or crushed burdock roots and leaves, infusion of walnut leaves (acts as a sedative and counteracts skin parasites), yeast taken orally (for the beauty of the skin).

Crazy for Cats

WALRUS AND THE SMITS FAMILY

My cat has got no name
We simply call him Cat;
He doesn't seem to blame
Anyone for that.

For he is not like us
Who often, I'm afraid,
Kick up quite a fuss
If our names are mislaid.

(Vernon Scannell)

* * *

The name is important; because while it is said that one ends up with the appearance one deserves, it is also true that one ends up by becoming one's own name. A great painter once said that it is only in trying to be a genius that there is a risk of becoming one. And in the *Tao Te-Ching*, the great Chinese book, we find the warning 'The name is the cause of all things'.

So to hear yourself called Puss Puss Puss Pussy is depressing. A dignified name augments any innate dignity, while an ordinary name makes a cat docile, and a pompous name, when lived up to, can confer authority.

However, never commit the error of calling a black cat Blackie, or a faithful dog Fido, because cats never change their colour and all dogs are faithful.

Sofia Luviska is just the name for a slim little thing, blonde with green slanting eyes, and a grey creature, pale like a northern sky, can respond only to the shining name of Clarissa.

A family of Siamese would be proud of Smits as a surname, and a Norwegian cat with a poor coat might improve if he was called Balloon.

Polly Molly, if she hasn't already a bouncy gait, will soon acquire one, and to be called Walrus would make the whiskers grow.

CRAZY FOR CATS

LADY LUSTI VON MIMOSEN

Loved by all
Is a well-dressed cat
She may strike you as dumb
But she knows where she's at
When she's stalking the cat walk
In Paris or Rome
She purrs with contentment
And feels most at home.

* * *

During the last November collections in Paris two models of extreme interest to big cats were shown: the flared poncho and the poncho pants. There were also two reduced sizes intended for small cats.

Four square metres of brushed wool are required for the flared poncho, its colours sober yet refined, pearl grey or sea blue for the gingers, blue-green for tabbies and stripey cats, white for the tortoiseshells and brown for the Siamese, with 16 metres of silk braid for the border. Cut the material in a circle, open a large hole in the centre for the head, and two smaller ones for the paws, and hem it all neatly. For those who feel the cold, a coloured belt can pull it in tight at the waist, holding it close to the body.

Other designs of interest: a little short-sleeved sweater in pure wool, dusty pink, sea green and ivory for the short hairs, a waxed raincoat for travelling in bad weather, a Sherlock Holmes deerstalker with a chinstrap against the wind, and a wide assortment of fancy collars and ceremonial ribbons.

Centre of public attention on account of her emerald necklace and ring, which she always wears to reflect her eyes, was Lady Lusti von Mimosen.

Crazy for Cats

ANNA LISA

*The sea's all right
It's not all salt
There's mullet red and mullet grey
And even turtles too they say.
I'm not against all liquids
Slimy though they be
But catch me unawares
And from the wet I'll flee.*

* * *

She does not like it in great quantities, warm, cold, hot or freezing; and going to the beach is not her favourite pastime. But, being red-haired, in summer she contents herself with just a light tan. It is not even any use for washing herself, though she is extremely conscientious in her cleanliness, and to overlook even the tiniest speck on her fur would worry her. In practice she considers it only useful for drinking; a small bowl full of fresh water should therefore be placed in a safe, separate place, because ancient memories tell her that the moment of drinking at the spring is the most dangerous, the moment the Great Big Enemy will choose for the ambush.

She mustn't forget that her ancestors, forced to jump on board ships in order to keep them free of mice, were great navigators, who traversed the oceans, in all weathers and even in storms. There are even some sporty and enterprising cats who like swimming. If necessary Anna Lisa will take a bath, but it is worth noting that when wet her fur, unlike that of a dog, loses its thermal protection and dries very slowly. Do her a favour therefore, and dry her carefully, and if it is necessary to use a hair dryer then make sure it's a silent one.

She has an interesting relationship with rain. She even has an advance warning system whereby before a shower her ears are charged with electricity, so she strokes them with her paw in order to relieve them. It seems then that there is a certain truth in the popular belief that a cat washing its ears with its paws means that rain is on its way.

35

CRAZY FOR CATS

DAISY AND HER KITTENS

I bathe it every night at nine,
I use it as a brolly
It swats the flies and sweeps the floor
It's really rather jolly.
In games it sometimes holds a bell
It even spreads my butter
How does a human being do
With hands and feet, of each, just two?

* * *

A noble extension of the dorsal spine, the tail is as indispensable to the cat as the cat is to the tail. It is not just an ornament which rounds off the splendid fur, but it is of constant practical use. It functions as a blanket in light winds, a balance for walking and dancing, a toy in early infancy or times of boredom and above all as a very effective means of expression: in such a way that we can define it as the terminal upon which are written the feelings and motives of the heart.

Language of the tail
Tail held straight and high: contentment, happy expectation, as when meeting a friend and accompanying him on a walk. A very annoyed cat will walk away with its tail held straight, thus demonstrating its independence and total indifference to whatever has happened.

Tail high, waving from side to side: joyous welcome.

Tail straight up but with the tip pointing forwards: profound satisfaction with his deeds.

Tail held low: shame, embarrassment, fear, terror.

Cat sitting or lying, with the tip of the tail twitching: boredom, restlessness, desire to be left undisturbed.

Tail half raised, tense: strong suspicion and preparation for an eventual attack.

Tail lashing from side to side in rapid and frequent movement: imminent violent and dangerous attack (the movement is accompanied by folded-back ears and terrifying growls).

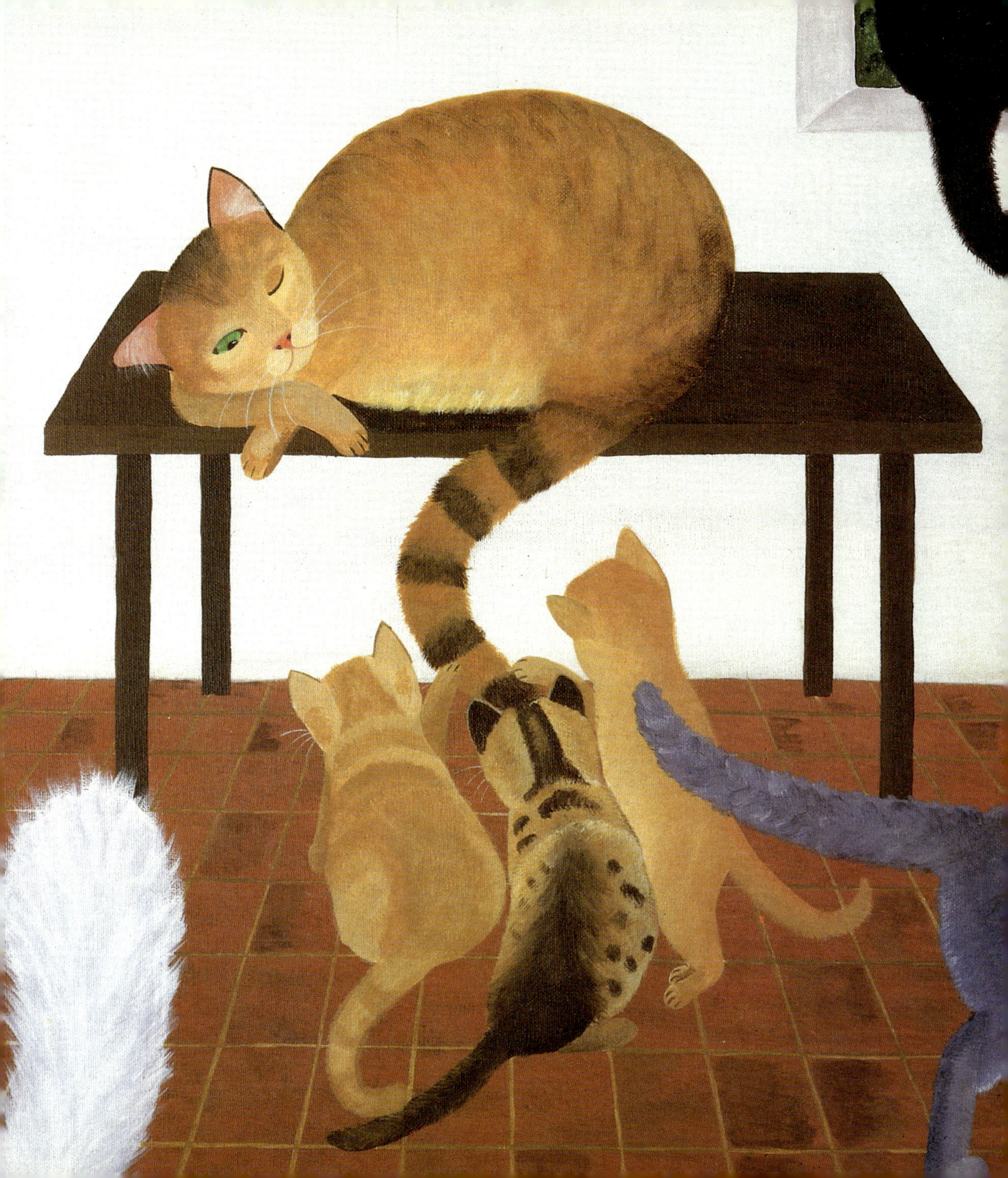

CRAZY FOR CATS

BILLY

She had a passion for scents. She would plunge her nose into bouquets and nibble a perfumed handkerchief with little paroxysms of delight. She would walk about on the dressing-table sniffing the stoppers of the scent-bottles, and she would have loved to use the violet powder if she had been allowed.

(Théophile Gautier)

* * *

If you want to give Billy a present of toilet water or a bunch of flowers, do remember that he has a marked preference for natural, sweet perfumes. The delicate fragrance of pumpkin flowers and even the more decisive scent of the pumpkin itself, is very pleasurable to him. Other perfumes and flowers which he likes are: lavender, mimosa, mint, carnation, sweet pea, asparagus, as well as, of course, catmint which sends him absolutely mad. Sometimes, other cats show an uncontrollable passion for the smell of bleach, or for sulphuric acid, or other concoctions of chemical origin, but these are personal preferences.

A much appreciated gesture is a gift of a catmint-stuffed mouse. To make one, you need a piece of printed cotton 25 x 15 centimetres, needle and thread, transparent nylon thread for the whiskers, two shiny black buttons, a little piece of cord for the tail, and dried catmint. Cut two mouse-shaped pieces and an oval for the base, and also two shapes like pairs of spectacles which when folded will give you the ears.

Sew the sides to the bottom, and to each other, leaving a little hole to put the stuffing in. Fold the spectacle shapes and fill them with a tiny amount of catmint, sew them up and fix them where mice usually have ears. Sew on the whiskers, eyes and tail.

39

CRAZY FOR CATS

TALKING HEADS

Talking heads, talking heads
They move their necks
And tap their feet.
In vain one wonders what they bleat.

* * *

A musical animal, if ever there was one, would be able to perfectly distinguish between a noise caused by irregular waves, and the sound produced by periodic vibrations, and music proper, which is beautiful because (in case you didn't know) it is formed by superimposed sinusoid curves. Not only that, but the cat manages to perceive sound of 40,000 hertz, and that corresponds to the patter of a little mouse on his tiny velvet paws, or the rustle of a caterpillar on a leaf – noises we simply cannot hear. (Nor can white cats with blue eyes, by the way, for they are deaf.)

Loving music does not only mean listening to it, but also making it. Cats usually contribute to the national melodic heritage with their voices, but there have been more inspired musicians, like the cat that belonged to Domenico Scarlatti who, walking on the piano keys, composed what his master entitled 'Fugue in Tempo Moderato' (The Cat Fugue).

To hear music clearly and gain maximum satisfaction (for music is one of a cat's greatest pleasures), they must hold their ears well-pricked and never turn them back towards the tail as this indicates mistrust.

41

CRAZY FOR CATS

P O L O A N D P E P P E R M I N T

*'Miaow miaow?' asked Peppermint
    this morning,
She is polite, refined and never
    fawning.
I was taking tea, but I had to say
    'Sorry,
I'm afraid there's no butter; why not
Have cake, or a biscuit or honey?'
'Mew mew?' asked Peppermint.
'No, it's not raining yet
But you'd better take an umbrella
To be safe, and not wet.'*

* * *

When you are invited into a friend's garden to play and there are other friends there too – like three little birds, for example – it is fundamentally important not to be inexperienced in the art of conversation, an art which permits an exchange of points of view.

The basis for a good conversation is a rich and varied vocabulary. Apart from purring, which is pretty limited and only expresses a short-lived satisfaction, Polo and Peppermint have at their disposal an extensive range of sounds. There are about sixty different miaows, each with its variation of intensity and tonality. E flat minor, suitable for communicating a delicate and sad state of mind, is completely different from C major which is the note for command and affirmation.

Anger and love are the sentiments which one is usually wanting to communicate, but do not underestimate the great need for a dialogue which touches on other matters, a need which is common to almost all beasts of every climate, civilization and epoch.

Conversation among those of the same race is very lively, but that between man and cat can also be fascinating. If a man can use the correct tones and not be patronizing, he will always receive satisfactory replies, and usually the cat will like to have the last word.

When Polo and Peppermint exhaust the possibilities of language, they resort to gestures: arching their backs, waving their tails, making their fur stand on end and moving their ears in all directions.

43

CRAZY FOR CATS

LOTS OF CATS

Our best companions have no fewer than four paws
(Colette)

I have noticed that what cats most appreciate in a human being is not the ability to produce food which they take for granted – but his or her entertainment value.
(Geoffrey Household)

* * *

Anyone with one cat always wants another, and anyone with two always wants a third and so on, because for people with a passion there is nothing more satisfying than being able to increase your collection. There are thirty-five breeds of domestic cats, with forty variations so there is plenty of choice. About fifteen is a good number to start with. Caring for lots of animals does the health and the spirit good. You forget your own problems; you don't have time for existential worries; you have to exercise patience, practise justice, firmness and democracy. You learn to settle disputes, placate jealousy and envy, distribute fairly love and caresses, though being quite aware that this does not give you a right to possess nor any right to expect reciprocation.

Notwithstanding belief to the contrary, a cat does not like being an only child. He knows that it is written in the Bible: 'Woe to him that is alone when he falleth, for he hath not another to help him up.' For this reason, he likes his peers, and man, and is capable of profound friendships.

There are many moving tales from all over the world, of emotional and unusual ties between cats and other animals of all kinds and social backgrounds: tortoises, horses, gorillas, and even elephants, guinea pigs, white mice and rabbits, and, still more unlikely, little birds. It is important, however, that introductions are made when the animals are of a tender age, before they have been able to form prejudices.

45

PHILIP AND THE BARN OWL

For the first week
Eat bananas
In the second, honey will do
(Though you may decide to eat this
Watching TV as you chew)
In week three, try some boiled fish;
In the fourth a veg or two
And perhaps a little cheese dish
Would not be completely taboo.
Now you'll find
That such a diet
Prescribed by Dr Mouse,
Will lead to feline herbivores
Who'll stay safe in the house.

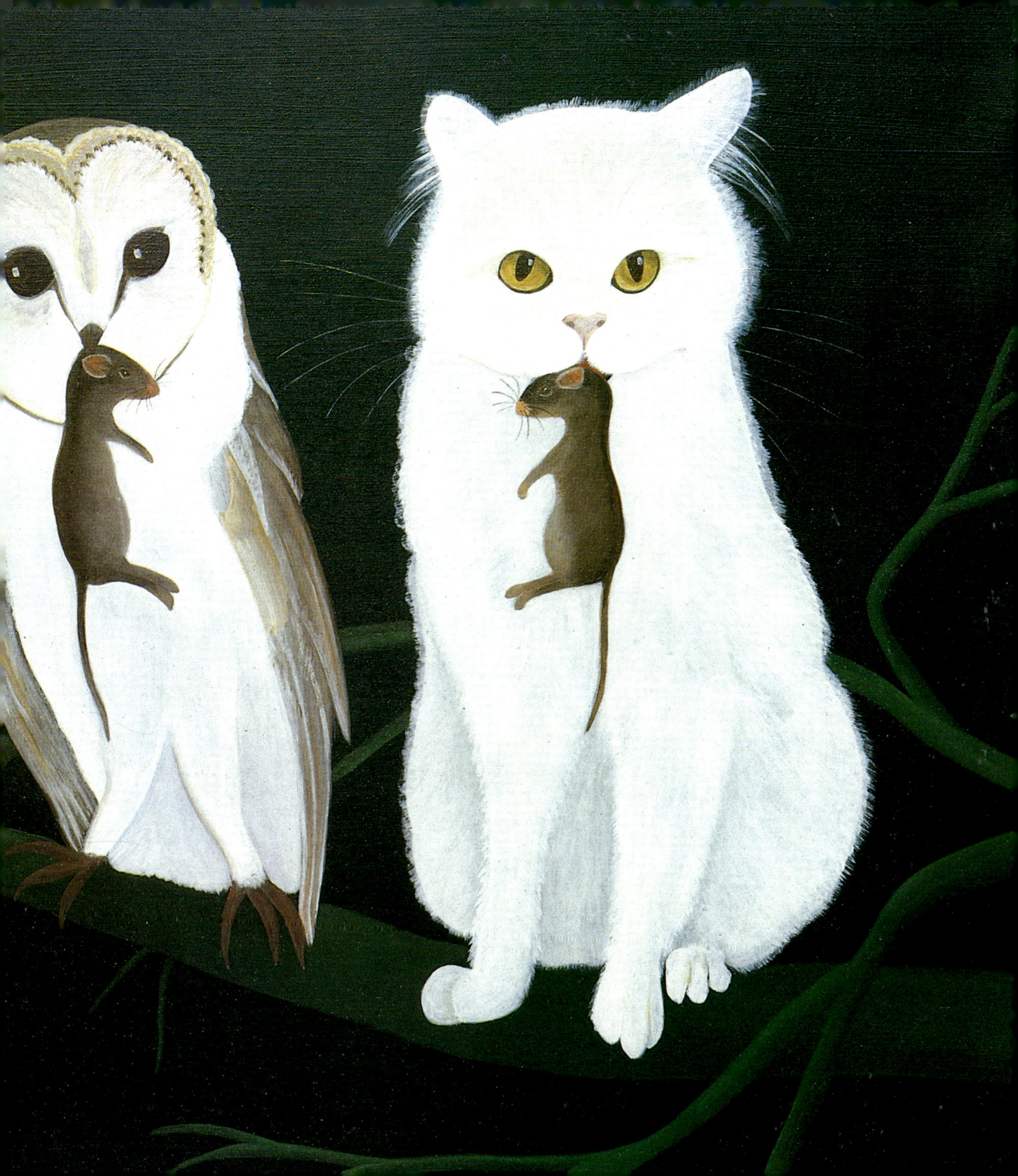

Crazy for Cats

PHILIP AND THE BARN OWL

Having phosphorescent eyes is great for going hunting by night with a barn owl. Philip is so luminous that he is used as a lantern.

When he has caught a mouse, you must not speak to him like a disobedient child. Philip knows that everyone kills for food, and judges it normal to be a carnivore. He is always very proud of his ability and he rarely fails to bring his prey home to show his dearest friend; he will deposit it on the drawing-room carpet, or on the doormat.

It is important to give him a word of praise, in order to consolidate the relationship between man and cat. To outrage him with an unjust reproof is a mistake, showing an unforgivable lack of sensitivity. All the same, if you are very compassionate and know for a fact that Philip is well-nourished, and goes hunting only because it is his instinct, you could provide nearby a special mouse wall, and endeavour to rescue those *in extremis*.

When Philip arrives triumphant, his mouse will almost always still be alive. You can thus proceed to open wide his jaws (not the mouse's naturally), while you are distracting him with sincere compliments in a soothing voice. Then you catch hold of the little mouse, who generally won't bite, and who is sure to be very clean, soft and pleasant to the touch. This is *not* a heroic act. Then you must go, as fast as you can, to the mouse wall, which should be loosely built, with lots of holes, cracks and cavities, and you liberate the poor creature. Usually the little things are absolutely terrified, but immensely grateful, and they will squeak a word of thanks before disappearing.

ROMA AND JULIUS

Dear Teresa

I don't know what is happening to me, but for a little while I have been howling at night if I see a little wall or a bush. When there is a moon I want to sleep on top of it, and, I am ashamed to say, at night I push over the dustbins. You are more expert than me, tell me: is this love?

Tosca

(Giovanni Gandini)

Roma and Julius are not confusing their sex, the biological trap laid for the conservation of the species, with love, which is immense, and without scope. Roma and Julius can be very faithful, are constant in friendship and love, which transcends the sexual act, which itself takes place without complications or prejudices (apart from the interference of man to prevent undesirable contacts), and indeed takes place with anyone whatever. Such clarity of intent eliminates the nuisance of jealousy and makes the behaviour more rational.

If sometimes love and friendship should cease, that's just human. But normally they last for life as far as cats are concerned, whether they turn to a fellow cat, man, or to another object, animate or inanimate.

Events connected with sex and love are generally passionate or romantic. Courtship, for example, is sweet, devoid of impatience, sacred like a rite, and rhythmic like a dance. The act of copulation is on the other hand ugly and slightly ridiculous, but it makes no exceptions and, as has been said, has its

ROMA AND JULIUS

limitations. Birth is moving, as is the care of a mother for her babies. To judge from the violence of the licks that she distributes, she knows the intensity of maternal love, devoted and selfless, but without sentimentality. Roma knows perfectly well that it's a fixed time contract.

Even among cats, there have been cases of reprehensible conduct, but as usual the exception proves the rule. If a mother, in a moment of bewilderment, cannot care for her kittens, or abandons them for a *force majeure*, it is useful to know that you can turn to bottle feeding by means of a syringe (obviously without the needle). You can buy enriched milk from a chemist, or use normal cow's milk, warmed, with a small amount of egg yolk and sugar.

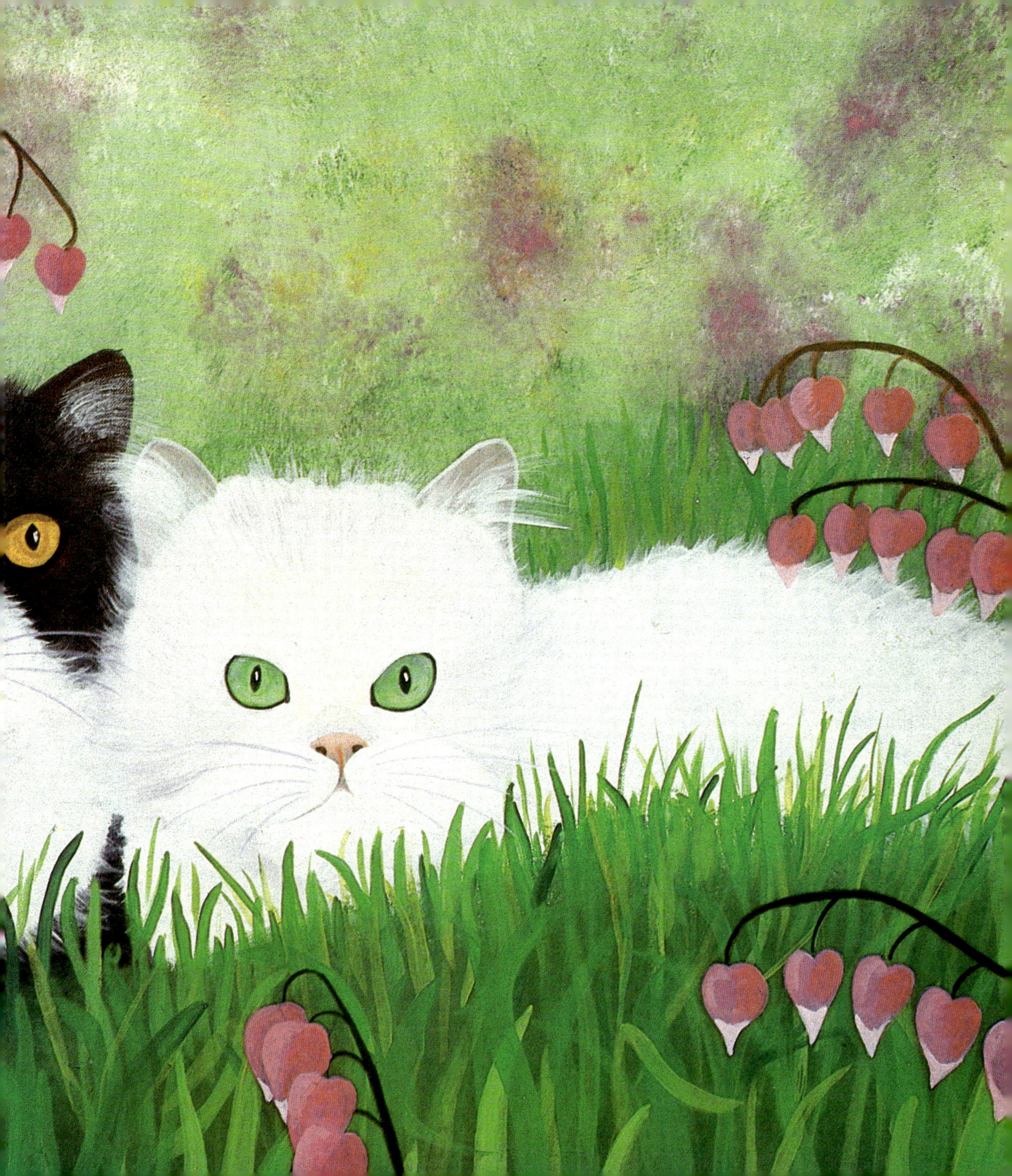

FURRY BEAR

The ignorant cat
Who's not been to school
Is really rather a stupid fool.
He's the sort of cat
Who can't even deduce
That an elephant's shape
Is not that of a goose.
He wonders where zebras
Buy stripey T-shirts
Not sure if a snake bite
Is pleasant or hurts.
And although he's seen Furry Bear
He can't really tell
If he's a Peruvian llama
Or a Thompson's gazelle.
If you live in a library
And look in a book
And work out that camels
Don't come from Innsbruck,
Then your difference in station
From that stupid cat
Would probably make you an
   aristocrat.

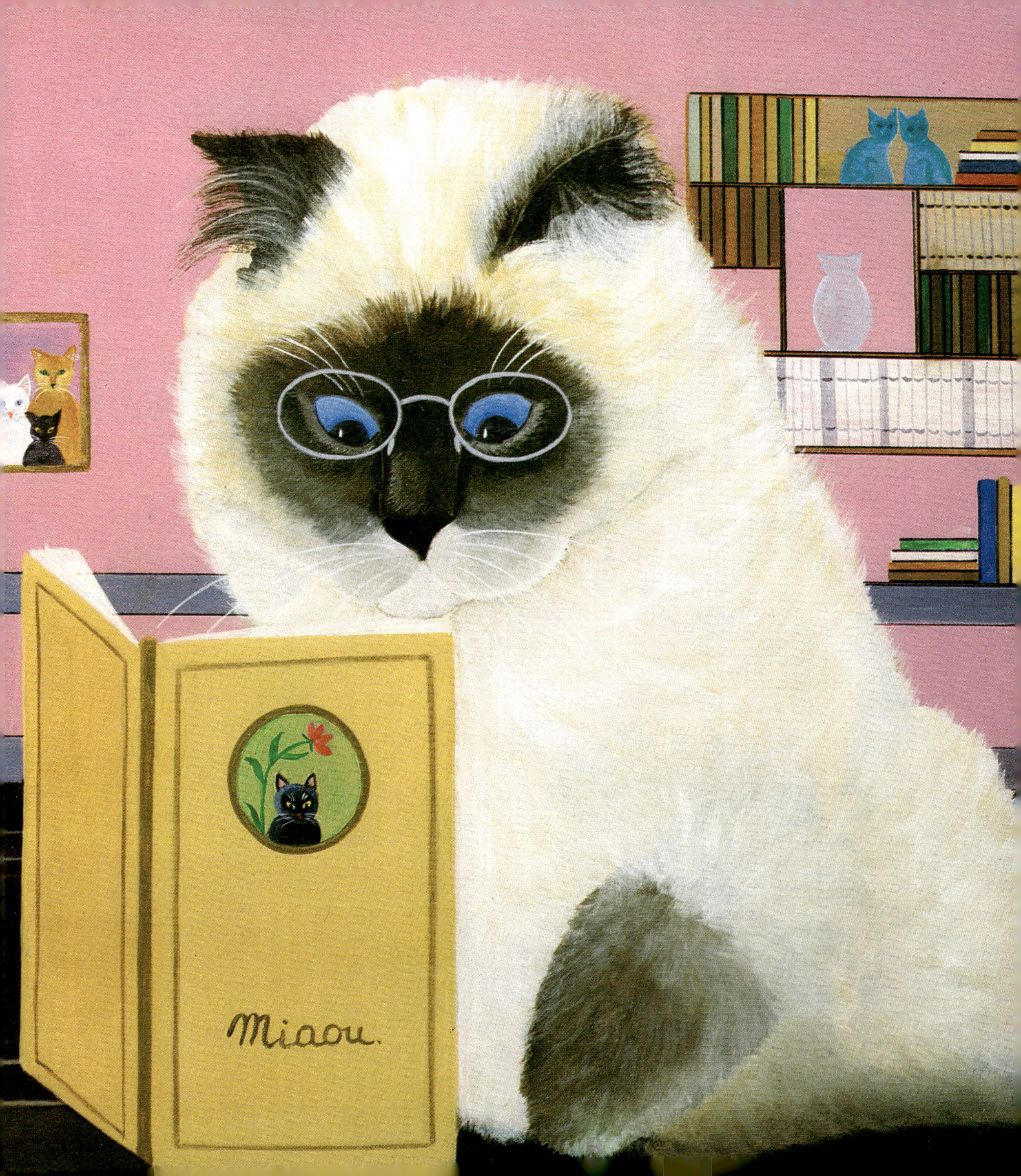
Miaou.

Crazy for Cats

FURRY BEAR

Furry Bear is not rash. When he does a thing, he does it well. Having in his youth had the opportunity to live in a library, he has realized the immensity and profundity of Knowledge. He has now graduated in ethnology, and is on the point of publishing his great popular scientific work, entitled *Quadrupeds*. It deals with a systematic catalogue of breeds of superior quadrupeds. To give an idea of the breadth of view and methodology of Furry Bear, we will mention his treatment of mice, skilfully divided into three classifications: pale brown, dark brown and stripey. The praiseworthy precision is such that all three are presented in subdivisions according to whether they have long or turned-up noses.

For the cat family, apart from an initial division for convenience into show cats and domestic cats, and apart from some minor or rare breeds in the appendix (Manx cats, cats with rabbits' tails, cats without tails), Furry Bear follows the most recent classification. This specifies a distinct watershed between short hair and long hair, and proceeds to describe the groups as follows:

Short haired
a) *Abyssinian*: very faithful, very sporty and lovers of mountaineering.
b) *Siamese*: long thin bodies with long legs; marvellous blue eyes, voice like sheep; pale coat with black gloves.
c) *Korats*: originally from Thailand; thick glossy silver-blue coat. Very large luminous green eyes. Likes a calm atmosphere.

d) *Burmese*: Asiatic charm; brown coat, sometimes grey, lilac or cream.
e) *Russian Blue*: pointed nose, green oval eyes; very aristocratic.
f) *European*: lovable for their friendliness, versatility, vivacity and intelligence; in many colours, black, white, brown, tortoiseshell, ginger, striped, tabby and bi-coloured.
g) *Cornish Rex*: these are cats even if they seem to be lambs; curly coats and even curly whiskers.

Long Haired
a) *Simple Persian*: very luxurious, everything concentrated on the appearance; mono-coloured (white with blue eyes, white with orange eyes, black, blue, cream, silver or red) and bi-coloured with the above mentioned tones.
b) *Persian Colourpoints*: (where points refers to the points of excellence in the beauty of the fur, or perhaps to the fact that they have fur of one colour with points – that is the mask, legs and tail – of another); special colouration: blue, chocolate and tortoiseshell.
c) *Birman*: majestic beauty; colour like the Siamese but with very long hair and white paws; sapphire eyes; highly affectionate but excessive sexual activity.
d) *Norwegian*: wild cats from the Scandinavian forests, capable of withstanding considerable cold thanks to a thick and woolly coat. Extraordinarily robust and adaptable.

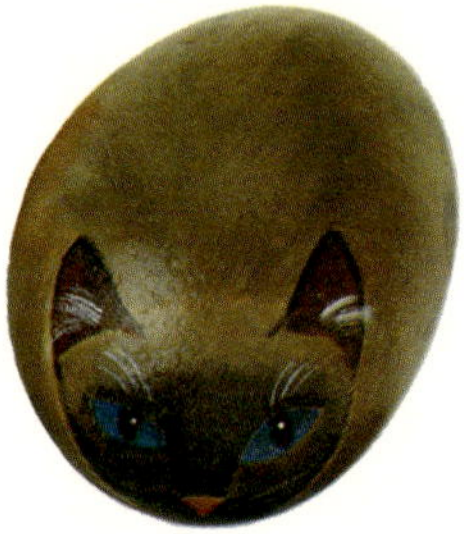

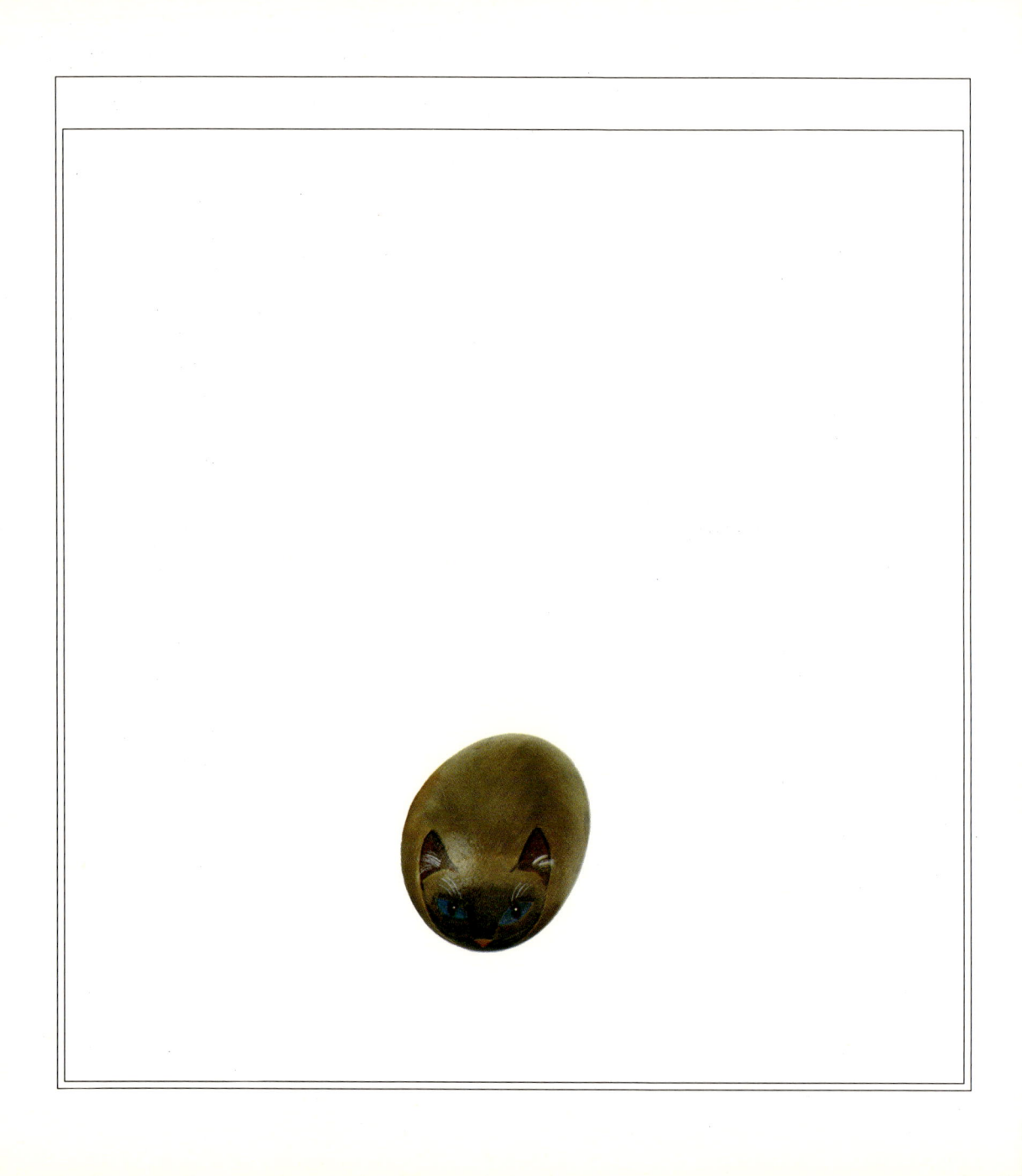